the Easy Way

ide to
he Northeast

Lynn Levine

Illustrated by Briony Morrow-Cribbs

Dedicated to:

Don Lubin, for sharing his extraordinary expertise in such an exceptionally open and supportive way. http://nefern.info

Cliff Adler, my husband, for his tireless commitment to the editing of this book.

- Lynn Levine

―――――――――

Helen O'Donnell, for her undying friendship and for always sharing her love of plants, both tame and wild.

- Briony Morrow-Cribbs

Identifying Ferns the Easy Way:
A Pocket Guide to the Common Ferns of the Northeast
Copyright © 2019 Lynn Levine
ISBN: 978-0-9703654-6-0

CONTENTS

HOW TO USE THIS GUIDE

Here are several approaches:

- When you look at a fern, you can determine which group (0 to 5) the fern belongs to based upon:
  - Structure (pp. 8-9)
  - Silhouettes (pp. 10-17)

- The individual species (pp. 18-71) are organized by group. Within each group, the ferns are arranged alphabetically. Each species has "Tips for Identification." The key characteristics to help you identify each fern are indicated by this symbol: ▶

- You can begin by observing where the ferns are growing. This will help you with over half of the ferns. See below for those that typically live in a specific environment.

Moist Habitat Ferns:

Cinnamon, Crested Wood, Marsh, Massachusetts, Ostrich, Royal and Sensitive

Rocky Habitat Ferns:

Bulblet, Ebony Spleenwort, Fragile, Rusty Woodsia, Marginal, Maidenhair Spleenwort and Rock Polypody

Fertile Habitat Ferns:

Maidenhair

This fern often grows with early spring wildflowers such as hepatica, ginger, leeks or Dutchman's Breeches.

Other ferns can grow almost anywhere.

GENERAL TIPS

- Not all ferns emerge at the same time of the year.

- Ferns that usually grow in clusters will sometimes grow alone. For example, you can find a single Interrupted Fern that is not in a cluster. Spend time to look around for variations.

- Longer or unusual fronds are generally the fertile ones (those with clusters of spore cases).

- For a few ferns, if you are having difficulty identifying them, look in another group. For example, the Sensitive Fern is in Group 1, but it almost looks like a Group 2 fern.

- Young ferns may not show all traits of mature ferns.

OBSERVING FERNS

When looking at ferns, it can be helpful to do more than just identify them.

For example, ask yourself:

- What are the differences & similarities between nearby ferns?

- What will the fern look like in a day, a week, a month?

- What did it look like a day, a week, a month ago?

- What can I discover using a magnifying lens?

- Does the stalk have a groove?

- Does the stalk have scales?

- What color is the stalk?

FERNS – ANCIENT PLANTS

Ferns have a very long and fascinating history. They first appeared 400 million years ago.

The blue-green algae (cyanobacteria) that lived everywhere on our ancient planet produced more and more oxygen, as did the ferns themselves. Ancestors of today's ferns and clubmosses grew and became as tall as trees. At that time, the oxygen increased to 35% of the atmosphere, the highest level ever! Currently, it is 21%. This oxygen allowed animals to emerge from the oceans and colonize the land. As the ferns died, toppled, washed into swamps and were buried In mud, over time they became the coal of today. Eventually, these large ferns went extinct.

About 250 million years ago there was a mass extinction on Earth and less than 10% of all life forms survived. Fern spores of surviving species dispersed widely, allowing those ferns to recover.

Fossil records show us that present-day ferns, Cinnamon Fern, Interrupted Fern and Royal Fern, were growing at least 200 million years ago.

Another mass extinction occurred 65 million years ago. This was when the dinosaurs died out, but ferns were among the survivors. For some time afterwards, flower pollen nearly disappeared, replaced almost entirely by fern spores.

FERNS – ANCIENT PLANTS

Scientists only recently discovered that, after flowering (broad-leaved) trees were re-established, ferns were threatened by shading from those trees. Evolution led to a genetic modification that allowed ferns to "capture" a specific gene from a mosslike plant. This extra gene provided ferns with the ability to absorb a broader color spectrum of light. This access to more light allowed ferns to successfully grow in shade.

Presently, there are an estimated 12,000 species of ferns worldwide.

Ferns are some of the oldest surviving plants with a:

- Vascular system – This allows ferns to transport water and nutrients from the soil.

- Physical support system containing lignin – This allows cells to have durable walls which provide stability.

These traits allowed ferns to grow tall.

REPRODUCTIVE SYSTEM

Ferns (along with mosses and horsetails) have a remarkable reproductive system. It was not until the late 1700s that scientists understood that these plants have two alternating phases to their life cycle!

One phase of the life cycle occurs when it is a **Sporophyte**. This is when it is the familiar looking plant with roots, stalk and leaves that we think of as "a fern." As its scientific name implies, a **Sporophyte** produces spores, which disperse, mostly by the wind and, if successful, develop into tiny new organisms.

The new organism, a **Gametophyte**, is the other phase of the life cycle. It is heart-shaped and is a totally independent organism, with its own root-like system. It is only clearly visible with a magnifying lens, since it is just ¼ inch in size.

If you had a microscope, you could see that the **Gametophyte** has male and female sex organs. **Gametophyte** is of Greek origin. *Gameto* means "to marry." *Phyte* means "plant."

Just as in animals, the male sex organ produces sperm. The sperm swim to a female sex organ and fertilize its egg. The result is an embryo.

The embryo grows into a new **Sporophyte**. The cycle is now complete and ready to begin again!

Vegetative Reproduction is another way for ferns to regenerate. The rhizome (page 9) elongates and new fronds can grow from it. Species having long and branching rhizomes may form large colonies of ferns.

FERN LIFE CYCLE

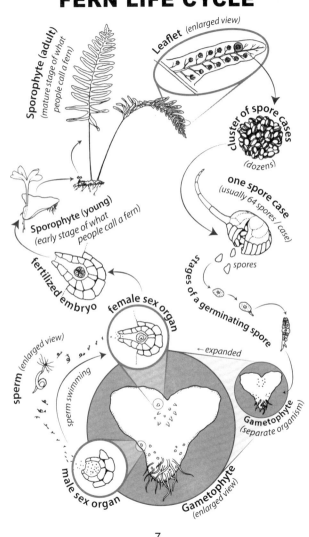

Sporophyte (adult) *(mature stage of what people call a fern)*

Leaflet *(enlarged view)*

cluster of spore cases *(dozens)*

one spore case *(usually 64 spores / case)*

spores

stages of a germinating spore

Sporophyte (young) *(early stage of what people call a fern)*

fertilized embryo

female sex organ

← expanded

sperm *(enlarged view)*

sperm swimming

Gametophyte *(separate organism)*

male sex organ

Gametophyte *(enlarged view)*

GROUP ILLUSTRATIONS

GROUP 0: NO-CUT

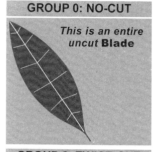

*This is an entire uncut **Blade***

GROUP 1: ONCE-CUT

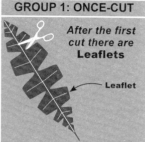

After the first cut there are **Leaflets**

Leaflet

GROUP 2: TWICE-CUT

After the second cut there are **Subleaflets**

Subleaflet

Leaflet

GROUP 3: THRICE-CUT

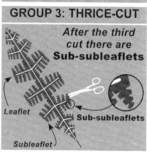

After the third cut there are **Sub-subleaflets**

Leaflet

Sub-subleaflets

Subleaflet

GROUP 4: THREE PARTS

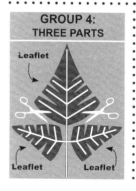

Leaflet

Leaflet   Leaflet

GROUP 5: UNIQUE

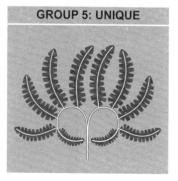

FERN PARTS & TERMS

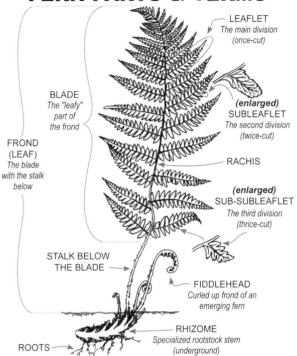

LEAFLET
*The main division
(once-cut)*

(enlarged)
SUBLEAFLET
*The second division
(twice-cut)*

BLADE
*The "leafy"
part of
the frond*

RACHIS

FROND
(LEAF)
*The blade
with the stalk
below*

(enlarged)
SUB-SUBLEAFLET
*The third division
(thrice-cut)*

STALK BELOW
THE BLADE

FIDDLEHEAD
*Curled up frond of an
emerging fern*

RHIZOME
*Specialized rootstock stem
(underground)*

ROOTS

Terms Used In _This_ Guide	Terms Used In _Other_ Guides
Blade	Lamina
Leaflet	Pinna
Subleaflet	Pinnule or Leafule
Sub-subleaflet	Pinnulet or Leaflet
Stalk below the blade	Stipe

SILHOUETTES

GROUP 1: ONCE-CUT

Christmas Fern
p. 18

Rock Polypody
p. 24

Sensitive Fern
p. 26

Ebony Spleenwort
p. 20

Maidenhair Spleenwort
p. 22

GROUP 2A
TWICE-CUT
VASE-LIKE CLUSTERS

Cinnamon Fern
p. 28

Interrupted Fern
p. 30

Marginal Wood Fern
p. 32

Ostrich Fern
p. 34

Royal Fern
p. 36

GROUP 2B
TWICE-CUT
NOT VASE-LIKE CLUSTERS

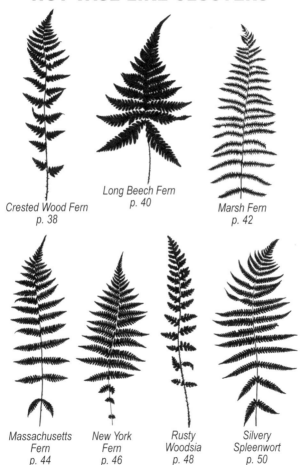

Crested Wood Fern
p. 38

Long Beech Fern
p. 40

Marsh Fern
p. 42

Massachusetts
Fern
p. 44

New York
Fern
p. 46

Rusty
Woodsia
p. 48

Silvery
Spleenwort
p. 50

GROUP 3: THRICE-CUT

Bulblet Fern
p. 52

Fragile Fern
p. 54

GROUP 3: THRICE-CUT

Hay-scented Fern
p. 56

Lady Fern
p. 58

Spinulose Wood Fern & Evergreen Wood Fern
p. 60

GROUP 4: THREE PARTS

Bracken Fern
p. 62

Cut-Leaf Grape Fern
p. 64

Oak Fern
p. 66

Rattlesnake Fern
p. 68

GROUP 5: UNIQUE

Maidenhair Fern
p. 70

Christmas Fern

(Polystichum acrostichoides)

Where it Grows:

- In forests, but rarely if the soil is very wet.

Tips for Identification:

- Fronds often grow in free-form clusters (rather than vase-like).
- Height of fern, at maturity, can be 2 to 3 feet.
- ▶ Fern stays green in all seasons and reminds us that spring will come again.
- Blade (the leafy part) is dark green and dramatically narrows toward the tip.
- ▶ Leaflets have a little bump (ear) near the stalk.
- Stalk below the blade is completely covered with scales.
- Fertile fronds, when present, have clusters of spore cases on the underside of the uppermost leaflets of these longer fronds.

Can be Confused With:

- Rock Polypody (p. 24), which also stays green in all seasons. One way to know the difference is that the Rock Polypody leaflets do not have the little bump (ear) near the stalk. Also, a Rock Polypody is much smaller than a mature Christmas Fern.

Interesting Notes:

- Used by early settlers for Christmas decorations.
- Provides good habitat in the winter for small mammals and ground nesting birds.
- Toxic to deer. Instead of eating this fern, deer are more likely to eat other nearby plants.

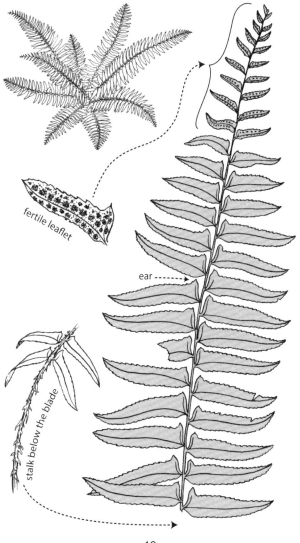

fertile leaflet

ear

stalk below the blade

Ebony Spleenwort
(Asplenium platyneuron)

Where it Grows:
- Most often found in rocky crevices, but can grow in a wide variety of shady conditions. *Not* a wetland plant.

Tips for Identification:
- Fronds usually grow in clusters.
- Height of fern, at maturity, can be 12 to 15 inches.
- Only the short fronds at the bottom of the fern stay green in all seasons. These short fronds form a rosette.
- ▶ Blade (the leafy part) is skinny and long.
- Leaflets have a little bump (ear) near the stalk.
- ▶ Leaflet pairs are alternate.
- ▶ Stalk is dark brown or black, shiny and smooth.
- Fertile fronds, when present, have clusters of spore cases which grow on their underside.

Can be Confused With:
- Maidenhair Spleenwort (p. 22), which has leaflets that *do not* have the little bump (ear) and has leaflet pairs that are opposite each other (like a bow tie).

Interesting Notes:
- Ebony Spleenwort gets the first part of its common name because the entire stalk turns a shiny black when it ages.
- Once thought (as with all spleenworts) to cure a diseased spleen, but this was found *not* to be true.
- New buds form at the base of the stalk which, if covered by soil, can grow into a new plant.

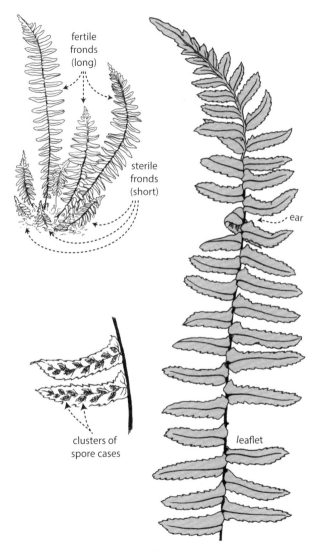

fertile
fronds
(long)

sterile
fronds
(short)

clusters of
spore cases

ear

*l*eaflet

Maidenhair Spleenwort

(Asplenium trichomanes)

Where it Grows:

- Rocky areas.
- It often grows along with moss in calcium rich areas.

Tips for Identification:

▶ Fronds usually grow in tight clusters.
- Frond length, at maturity, is about 2 to 5 inches.
- Fern stays green in all seasons.
- Blade (the leafy part) is ribbon-like and the tip narrows.
- Leaflets are semi-oblong (like a stretched out circle).

▶ Leaflet pairs are opposite each other (like a bow tie).
- Stalk is purple-brown, shiny and smooth.
- Fertile fronds, when present, have clusters of spore cases which grow on their underside.

Can be Confused With:

- Ebony Spleenwort (p. 20), though that fern has a little bump (ear) and its leaflet pairs are alternate.
- There is another virtually identical Maidenhair Spleenwort, *Asplenium quadrivaens,* (not included in this guide). They can be distinguished only by differences in spore size and the type of rock they grow on.

Interesting Notes:

- Range is almost worldwide.
- *Trichomanes* is the ancient Greek word meaning "hair of the head," probably from *tricho* which means hairy and *manes* which means flowing.
- As mentioned on page 20, it was once thought that all spleenworts could cure a diseased spleen, but this was found *not* to be true.

22

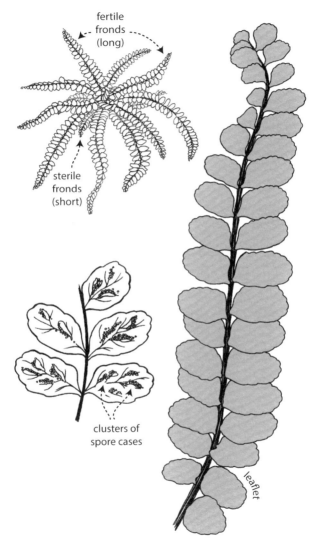

fertile fronds (long)

sterile fronds (short)

clusters of spore cases

leaflet

23

Rock Polypody

(Polypodium virginianum)

Where it Grows:

- Commonly found on exposed rocky surfaces.

Tips for Identification:

- Fronds often grow mat-like (like grass).
- Height of fern, at maturity, can be 8 inches.
- Fern stays green in all seasons.
- Blade (the leafy part) narrows toward the tip.
- ▶ Leaflets are elongated, have smooth edges and flare where they meet the stalk.
- ▶ Leaflet pairs are alternate.
- Fertile fronds, when present, have clusters of spore cases that are brown and grow on the underside of the uppermost leaflets.

Can be Confused With:

- Christmas Fern (p. 18), which also stays green in all seasons. One way to know the difference is that the Christmas Fern leaflets have the little bump (ear) near the stalk . Also, a mature Christmas Fern is much larger than a Rock Polypody.
- Appalachian Polypody (not included in this guide),which is widest near the base and has leaflets that are more pointy.

Interesting Notes:

- In Latin, *poly* means many and *pod* means foot. Rock Polypody has many "feet" connecting one fern to the next by their roots.
- Provides food, in extreme winter temperatures, for ruffed grouse, wild turkey and deer.

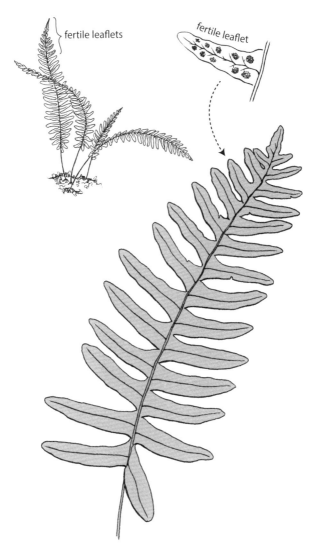

fertile leaflets

fertile leaflet

Sensitive Fern

(Onoclea sensibilis)

Where it Grows:

- Moist conditions in sun and shade.

Tips for Identification:

- Fronds may grow in large colonies.
- Height of fern, at maturity, can be 18 to 24 inches.
- Fern *does not* stay green in all seasons.
- ▶ Blade (the leafy part) is in the shape of a triangle.
- Topmost leaflets are smooth. The others have wavy edges, but are *not* cut deep enough to be considered twice-cut.
- Leaflet pairs are opposite each other (like a bow tie).
- Stalk within the blade (Rachis) is surrounded by leaf tissue.
- ▶ Fertile fronds, when present, have bead-like clusters growing on separate stalks (green at first and later turn brown). They can be seen throughout the winter if the snow is not too deep.

Can be Confused With:

- May look like the Group 2B ferns, except that the wavy edges are *not* deep enough to be considered twice-cut.

Interesting Notes:

- This fern, as its name suggests, is sensitive to the first frost.
- Known as "Bead Fern" due to the bead-like clusters on its fertile frond.
- Provides habitat for salamanders and frogs.
- It is an older species of fern that is 55 million years old.
- Toxic chemistry of this fern limits feeding by animals.

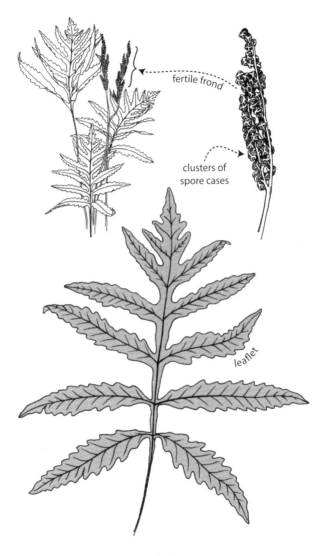

fertile frond

clusters of
spore cases

leaflet

27

Cinnamon Fern

(Osmundastrum cinnamomeum)

Group 2A

Where it Grows:

- In wet areas, including bogs, swamps and along stream banks.

Tips for Identification:

- Fronds grow in clusters, creating a vase-like shape.
- Height of fern, at maturity, can be 2 to 5 feet.
- Fern *does not* stay green in all seasons.
- Blade (the leafy part) is broadest at the center.
- ▶ Leaflets have tiny cinnamon-colored *woolly tufts* near the stalk.
- ▶ Leaflets are quite pointy.
- Stalk below the blade is brown, fuzzy and slightly grooved.
- ▶ Fertile fronds, when present, are separate stalks which are green at first and later become cinnamon-colored.

Can be Confused With:

- Interrupted Fern (p. 30), which has a less pointy blade tip, less pointy leaflets, and *does not* have the tiny cinnamon-colored *woolly tufts.*
- Ostrich Fern (p. 34), which has a significantly deeper groove along its stalk and *does not* have the cinnamon-colored *woolly tufts.*

Interesting Notes:

- It is named Cinnamon Fern, *not* because it tastes like cinnamon, but because of the color of its fertile fronds.

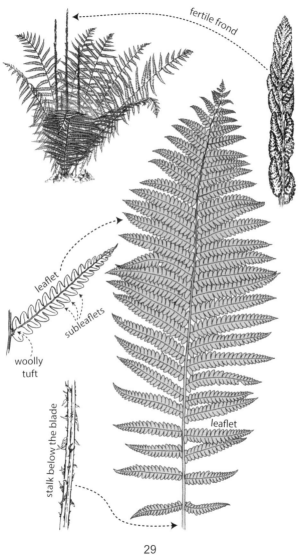

fertile frond

leaflet

subleaflets

woolly tuft

stalk below the blade

leaflet

29

Interrupted Fern
(Osmunda claytoniana)

Where it Grows:
- Both in wet and dry areas.

Tips for Identification:
- Fronds grow in clusters, creating a vase-like shape.
- Height of fern, at maturity, can be 2 to 5 feet.
- Fern *does not* stay green in all seasons.
- ▶ Subleaflets are rounded along the edge.
- Stalk is slightly grooved and *does not* have scales.
- ▶ Fertile fronds have leaflets covered with clusters of spore cases which are lacy, brown and symmetrical. In the spring, at a distance, these leaflet pairs look a bit like a tiny butterfly. Later in the season, the clusters of spore cases are dried and the leaflets hang down.

Can be Confused With:
- Cinnamon Fern (p. 28), which has a more pointy blade tip, more pointy leaflets, and tiny cinnamon-colored *woolly tufts*.
- Ostrich Fern (p. 34), which has a significantly deeper groove along its stalk.

Interesting Notes:
- Interrupted Fern gets its name from the fact that the fertile leaflets, when present, grow in the middle of the blade and "interrupt" the other leaflets.
- Its fiddleheads are stout, very woolly and brown. Unlike the Ostrich Fern, these are *NOT* edible.
- Interrupted Fern's fossil record places it as the earliest fern in eastern North America, dating back 200 million years. This is about three times earlier than when the dinosaurs became extinct.

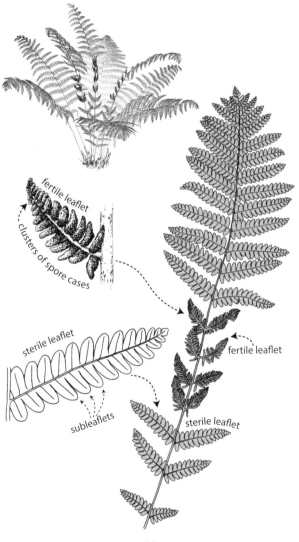

fertile leaflet

clusters of spore cases

sterile leaflet

subleaflets

fertile leaflet

sterile leaflet

31

Marginal Wood Fern

(Dryopteris marginalis)

Where it Grows:

- Rocky areas, almost always.

Tips for Identification:

- Fronds grow in clusters, creating a vase-like shape.
- Height of fern, at maturity, can be 3 feet or more.
- Fern stays green in all seasons and reminds us that spring will return.
- ▶ Blade (the leafy part) is leathery and blue-green, which really makes it stand out.
- Blade is widest near the middle.
- Subleaflets have wavy edges, but are *not* cut deep enough to be thrice-cut.
- Stalk below the blade is covered with ragged scales.
- ▶ Fertile fronds have clusters of spore cases which grow on the underside of the upper $\frac{2}{3}$ of the blade. Since the clusters of spore cases grow along the edges of the subleaflets, that is key to identifying this fern.

Can be Confused With:

- Many of the other vase-like shaped ferns (pp. 28-31 and 34-35), but no others are blue-green in color or leathery.

Interesting Notes:

- Sometimes called "Evergreen Fern," but this should not to be confused with Evergreen Wood Fern (p.60).
- It is called Marginal Wood Fern because its clusters of spore cases grow along the edges (the margins) of the subleaflets.

fertile leaflet

spore case clusters

subleaflets

fertile leaflet

stalk below the blade

33

Ostrich Fern

(Matteuccia struthiopteris)

Where it Grows:

- In wet areas, including wetlands, woodland springs and stream banks.

Tips for Identification:

- Fronds grow in clusters, creating a vase-like shape.
- Height of fern, at maturity, can be 5 feet (known to grow to 7 feet).
- Fern *does not* stay green in all seasons.
- ▶ Blade (the leafy part) is full at the top and then slowly narrows toward the bottom. This makes it look like an ostrich feather.
- Leaflets narrow to the tip.
- ▶ Stalk is deeply grooved. This is a very significant identification factor.
- ▶ Clusters of spore cases, when present, grow on a separate fertile stalk in the center of the "vase."

Can be Confused With:

- Cinnamon Fern (p. 28), which is only slightly grooved and has tiny cinnamon-colored *woolly tufts* near the stalk.
- Interrupted Fern (p. 30), which has a shallower groove along the stalk.

Interesting Notes:

- The Ostrich Fern is sometimes called "Fiddlehead Fern." Its fiddlehead is bright green and smooth. It is delicious when cooked.
- The fertile frond may remain standing during the winter.
- The Latin name *Struthos* comes from the Greek word meaning ostrich. *Pteris* means fern.

34

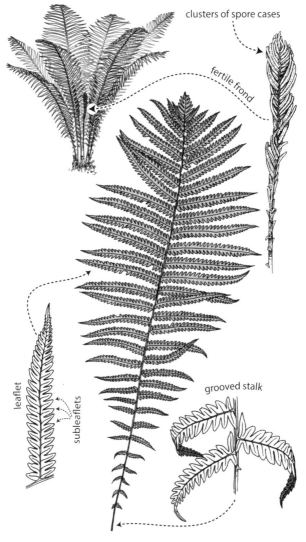

clusters of spore cases

fertile frond

leaflet

subleaflets

grooved stalk

35

Royal Fern

(Osmunda regalis)

Where it Grows:

- In wetlands (even if the water is deep) and in other wet areas.

Tips for Identification:

- Fronds grow in clusters, creating a vase-like shape.
- Height of fern, at maturity, can be 3 to 6 feet.
- Fern *does not* stay green in all seasons.
- ▶ Leaflets and subleaflets are widely spaced and the leaf has an "airy" appearance.
- Leaflet pairs are opposite each other (like a bow tie).
- Subleaflet pairs are alternate.
- ▶ Clusters of spore cases, when present, are located at the tip of a separate fertile frond.

Can be Confused With:

- Royal Fern is unlike any other fern. Sometimes, it is not even recognized as a fern.

Interesting Notes:

- It is sometimes called "Flowering Fern" since its separate fertile frond can look like a flower.
- A related variety grows in Europe, Asia and Africa.
- Roots are a source of fiber (osmundine) that is sometimes used as a growing medium for orchids.

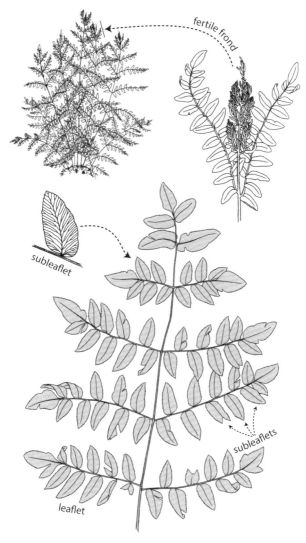

fertile frond

subleaflet

subleaflets

leaflet

Crested Wood Fern

(Dryopteris cristata)

Where it Grows:

- In wet or swampy areas. Tends to grow in shade.

Tips for Identification:

- Fronds grow in loose clusters.
- Height of fern, at maturity, can be 1 to 3 feet.
- Only the sterile fronds stay green in the winter. The fertile fronds may weaken at the bottom and fall over.
- Blade (the leafy part) is narrow.
▶ Leaflets on fertile fronds are "ladder-like."
- Lower pairs of leaflets are triangular in shape.
- Subleaflets *do not* reach the mid-vein.
▶ Stalk below the blade is covered with ragged scales.
- Fertile fronds, when present, have clusters of spore cases which grow on their underside.

Can be Confused With:

- None in particular.

Interesting Notes:

- This plant has been used as an antimicrobial agent. A root extract from Crested Wood Fern has been shown effective in expelling intestinal parasites from certain mammals.

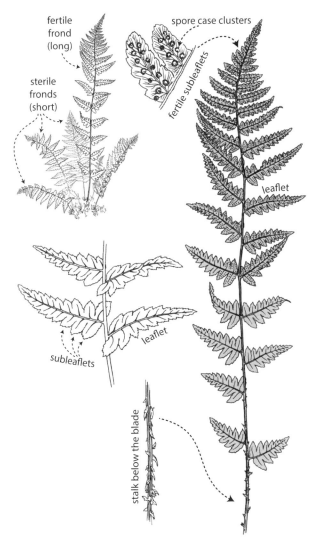

fertile frond (long)

sterile fronds (short)

spore case clusters

fertile subleaflets

leaflet

leaflet

subleaflets

stalk below the blade

Long Beech Fern

(Phegopteris connectilis)

Where it Grows:

- Throughout forested areas.

Tips for Identification:

- Fronds may grow in colonies.
- Height of fern, at maturity, can be 1 to 2 feet.
- Fern *does not* stay green in all seasons.
- ▶ Blade (the leafy part), above the bottom pair of leaflets, forms a triangular shape.
- ▶ Bottom pair of leaflets point down and forward (It feels like the fern is reaching out to you with open arms.)
- A "wing-like" structure connects leaflet pairs to each other at the stalk, except for the lowest 1 or 2 pairs.
- Fertile fronds, when present, have clusters of spore cases which grow on their underside.

Can be Confused With:

- Broad Beech Fern (Phegopteris hexagonoptera), which also has the wing-like structures connecting leaflet pairs to the stalk, but on this fern that continues all the way to the bottom pairs. This fern *is not* common enough to be included in this guide.

Interesting Notes:

- "Beech" is part of this fern's name because it can be found in woodlands where beech trees are growing.
- It is sometimes called "Northern Beech Fern" or "Narrow Beech Fern."

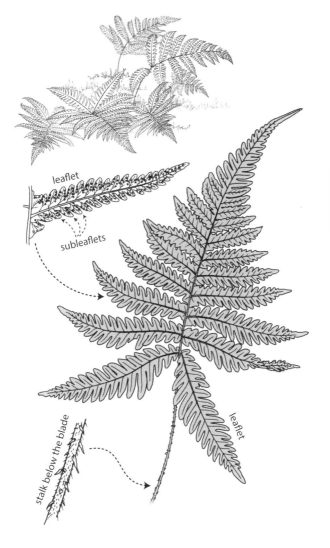

leaflet

subleaflets

stalk below the blade

leaflet

41

Marsh Fern

(Thelypteris palustris)

Where it Grows:

- As you might imagine from its common name, Marsh Fern grows in wet areas that are in sun or partial shade.

Tips for Identification:

- Fronds often grow in colonies.
- Height of fern, at maturity, can be 1 to 2½ feet.
- Fern *does not* stay green in all seasons.
- Blade (the leafy part) tears easily.
- ▶ Sterile and fertile fronds have very different appearances because, on the fertile leaflets, the subleaflets curl around the clusters of spore cases.
- ▶ Fertile leaflets may be twisted along their length.
- ▶ Lowest leaflet pair is perpendicular to the stalk.
- Fertile fronds, when present, have spore case clusters which grow on the underside of their upper leaflets.

Can be Confused With:

- Massachusetts Fern (p. 44), which has a bottom pair of leaflets that angle downward and forward.
- New York Fern (p. 46), which has leaflets that dramatically get shorter toward the bottom of the blade.
- Silvery Spleenwort (p. 50), which has a stalk with silvery hairs & silvery spore cases in a herringbone pattern.

Interesting Notes:

- Also grows in Europe and Asia.
- The caterpillars of the Marsh Fern Moth feed on the leaves of this fern. The Marsh Fern is the only known host plant of this uncommon moth.
- Since this fern often forms dense colonies, it provides good cover for smaller wildlife species.

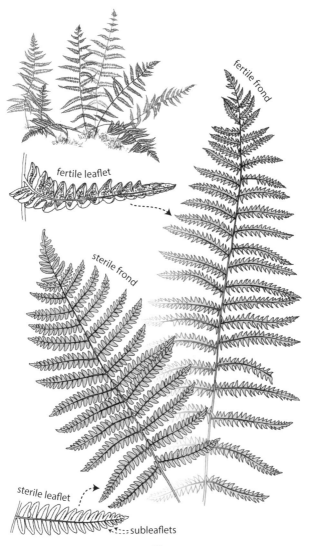

fertile frond

fertile leaflet

sterile frond

sterile leaflet

subleaflets

Massachusetts Fern

(Coryphopteris simulata)

Where it Grows:

- In wet areas.

Tips for Identification:

- Fronds may grow in clusters.
- Height of fern, at maturity, can be 1½ to 2½ feet.
- Fern *does not* stay green in all seasons.
- Blade (the leafy part) is oblong, with a point at the tip.
- Leaflets are narrow and separated along the stalk.
- ▶ Bottom pair of leaflets angle downward & forward.
- Leaflets have subleaflets with veins which have only a small amount of branching.
- On the lower leaflets, the subleaflets are narrower and smaller towards the stalk.
- Fertile fronds, when present, have spore case clusters which grow on the underside of their upper leaflets. On these leaflets, the subleaflets *do not* curl around the clusters of spore cases.

Can be Confused With:

- Marsh Fern (p. 42), which has a bottom pair of leaflets that are perpendicular to the stalk.
- New York Fern (p. 46), which has leaflets that get dramatically shorter toward the bottom.
- Silvery Spleenwort (p. 50), which has a stalk covered with silvery hairs and may have subleaflets with silvery spore case clusters in a distinctive herringbone pattern.

Interesting Notes:

- Named in 1894, which is later than most other ferns.
- *Simulata* means "resembling" other ferns.
- It is sometimes called "Bog Fern."

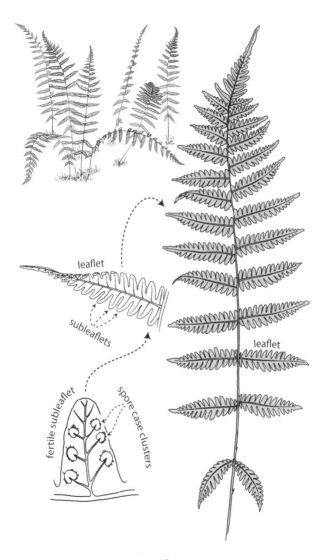

leaflet

subleaflets

fertile subleaflet

spore case clusters

leaflet

45

New York Fern

(Parathelypteris noveboracensis)

Where it Grows:

- Throughout the forest (including sunny patches).

Tips for Identification:

- Fronds tend to grow in large colonies. However, this fern often grows in clusters of just three or so fronds.
- Height of fern, at maturity, is 1 to 2 feet.
- Fern *does not* stay green in all seasons.
- ► Leaflets dramatically get shorter toward the bottom.
- Fertile fronds, when present, have clusters of spore cases which grow on their underside.

Can be Confused With:

- Marsh Fern (p. 42), which *does not* have lower leaflets that dramatically shorten.
- Massachusetts Fern (p. 44), which *does not* have lower leaflets that dramatically shorten.
- Silvery Spleenwort (p. 50), which has a stalk covered with silvery hairs and may have subleaflets with silvery spore case clusters in a distinctive herringbone pattern.

Interesting Notes:

- Dense understories of New York Fern, Hay-scented Fern or Bracken Fern can interfere with the regeneration of hardwood forests, threatening their sustainability.
- Notice the taper at the top and bottom. A humorous hint for remembering this fern is "When in New York, we always burn the candle at both ends."
- The caterpillars of the Pink-shaded Fern Moth feed on the leaves of this fern. An aphid, Amphorophora ampullata, feeds on its plant juices. Otherwise, this fern appears to be of low value to wildlife.

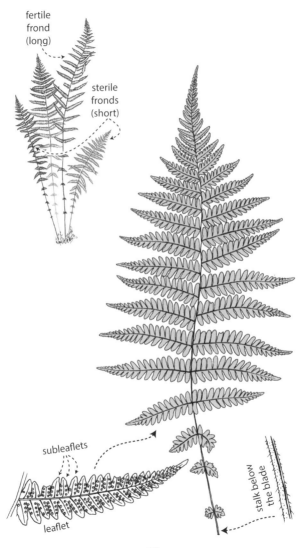

fertile frond (long)

sterile fronds (short)

subleaflets

leaflet

stalk below the blade

47

Rusty Woodsia
(Rusty Cliff Fern)
(Woodsia ilvensis)

Where it Grows:
- Rocky ledges which have a limited amount of moss.

Tips for Identification:
- Fronds grow in dense clusters.
- Height of fern, at maturity, is 4 to 8 inches.
- Fern *does not* generally stay green in all seasons. In sheltered areas it may overwinter.
- Blade (the leafy part) is green above and has silvery-white hairs on the underside.
- ▶ As this fern ages, the blade hairs become rusty in color.
- ▶ Blade is upright, brittle, pointed at the tip and slightly narrower at the bottom.
- Subleaflets are oval and slightly pointed.
- Fertile fronds, when present, have clusters of spore cases which grow on their underside, near the edges of the leaflets.

Can be Confused With:
- Bulblet Fern (p. 52), which *does not* have hairs on the underside of the blade.
- Fragile Fern (p. 54), which *does not* have hairs on the underside of the blade.

Interesting Notes:
- It is named Rusty Woodsia because the hairs on the leaflets, which are gray at first, become rusty in color as they age.
- It is sometimes called Hairy Woodsia.

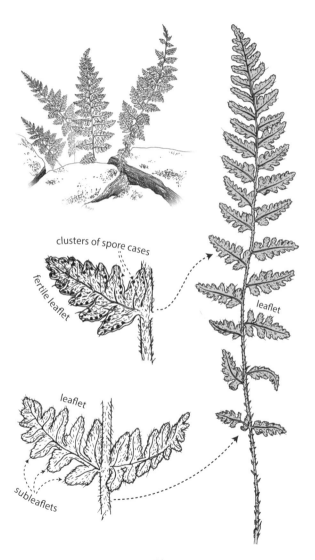

clusters of spore cases

fertile leaflet

leaflet

leaflet

subleaflets

49

Silvery Spleenwort
(Silvery Glade Fern) *(Deparia acrostichoides)*

Where it Grows:
- Throughout the forest.

Tips for Identification:
- Fronds grow in asymmetrical clusters.
- Frond is very delicate, for such a tall fern.
- Height of fern, at maturity, can be 2 to 3 feet.
- Fern *does not* stay green in all seasons.
- Leaflets get shorter toward the bottom.
- ▶ Lowest pair of leaflets point down.
- Stalk is covered with silvery hairs.
- ▶ Longest (fertile) fronds have clusters of spore cases which grow on their underside.
- Fertile fronds have silvery spore case clusters arranged in a distinctive herringbone pattern on their underside.

Can be Confused With:
- Marsh Fern (p. 42), which has bottom leaflets that are perpendicular to the stem and has clusters of spore cases that *do not* form a herringbone pattern.
- Massachusetts Fern (p. 44), with a stalk that *does not* have silvery hairs and has clusters of spore cases that *do not* form a herringbone pattern.
- New York Fern (p. 46), which has leaflets that dramatically get shorter toward the bottom, and has spore case clusters that *do not* form a herringbone pattern.

Interesting Notes:
- Named for the many silvery spore case clusters and hairs that give it a sheen in wind or sunlight. The spore case clusters can sometimes be seen through the leaf.

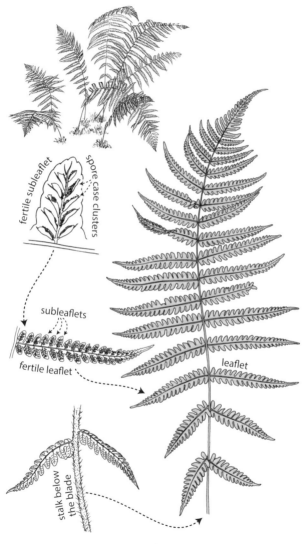

fertile subleaflet

spore case clusters

subleaflets

fertile leaflet

leaflet

stalk below the blade

Bulblet Fern

(Cystopteris bulbifera)

Where it Grows:

- Usually, hanging down on wet limestone rock faces which are often covered with moss.

Tips for Identification:

- Fronds grow in free-form clusters.
- Fern, at maturity, can be 1 to 2 feet in length.
- Fern *does not* stay green in all seasons.
- ▶ Blade (the leafy part) dramatically decreases in width toward the tip.
- Subleaflets are finely cut into sub-subleaflets.
- Fertile fronds, when present, have clusters of spore cases which grow on their underside, and away from their edges.
- ▶ Sometimes, on the underside of the blade, there are small green spherical bulblets attached to the stalk. These are usually split at the top.
- ▶ Bulblets turn dark when mature.

Can be Confused With:

- Fragile Fern (Brittle Fern) (p. 54), which is wider and never has bulblets.
- Rusty Woodsia (p. 48), which has hairs on the underside of the blade.

Interesting Notes:

- This fern can reproduce asexually (without spores). When a bulblet falls off or touches the ground, it may take root and grow into a brand new fern, which is a clone of its parent fern.
- It is one of the rare ferns that reproduces from bulblets.

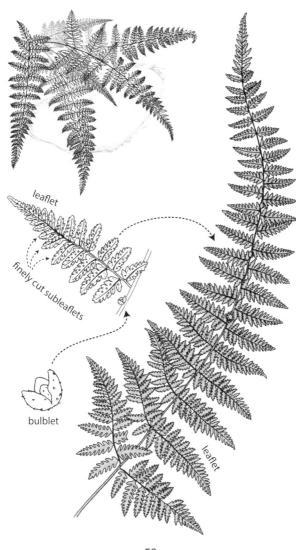

leaflet

finely cut subleaflets

bulblet

leaflet

Fragile Fern (Brittle Fern)

(Cystopteris fragilis)

Where it Grows:

- Usually in rock crevices, especially in the spring when there is water in the crevices. Often grows near moss.

Tips for Identification:

- Fronds grow in loosely formed groups.
- Fern, at maturity, can be $\frac{1}{2}$ to $1\frac{1}{2}$ feet in length.
- Fern *does not* stay green in all seasons.
- Leaflets are perpendicular to the stalk.
- Leaflets are widest towards the middle of the leaf.
- Subleaflets are finely cut into sub-subleaflets.
- ▶ Often, you can find last year's dead fronds hanging from the base of the fern.
- ▶ Stalk is dark brown or black near the ground.
- Fertile fronds, when present, have clusters of spore cases which are somewhat round and which grow on their underside.

Can be Confused With:

- Bulblet Fern (p. 52), which is narrower and sometimes has bulblets.
- Rusty Woodsia (p. 48), which has hairs on the underside of the blade.
- Mackay's Fragile Fern (not included in this guide), which has leaflets that tend to curl upwards.

Interesting Notes:

- As indicated by its name, this fern can be fragile and brittle to the touch.

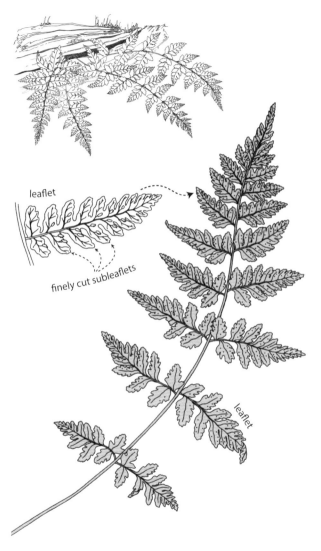

leaflet

finely cut subleaflets

leaflet

Hay-scented Fern

(Dennstaedtia punctilobula)

Where it Grows:

- Partial shade, sunny woods, roadsides, clearings and rocky slopes.

Tips for Identification:

- ▶ Single fronds tend to grow in large colonies.
- Height of fern, at maturity, can be 1 to 3 feet.
- Fern *does not* stay green in all seasons.
- Blade (the leafy part) is pointed at the tip, widest in the middle, and slowly gets narrower toward the bottom.
- Leaves smell like cut hay when they are broken.
- Subleaflets are finely cut into sub-subleaflets.
- ▶ Stalk below the blade is slender. It is brown or black, especially closer to the ground.
- Fertile fronds, when present, have spore case clusters which grow on their underside and are shaped like tiny cups.

Can be Confused With:

- Lady Fern (p. 58), which grows in clusters and has a stalk with dark brown scales.
- Spinulose & Evergreen Wood Ferns (p. 60), which have many scales on their stalks.

Interesting Notes:

- When its leaves are cut and dried, you can smell its strong sweet grasslike fragrance.
- Sensitive to early frosts, which can turn them white.
- The fronds can be used in cut flower arrangements.
- Dense understories of Hay-scented, New York or Bracken Fern can interfere with the regeneration of hardwood forests, threatening their sustainability.

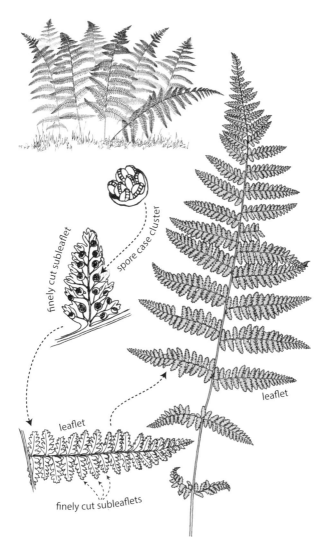

finely cut subleaflet

spore case cluster

leaflet

leaflet

finely cut subleaflets

57

Lady Fern

(Athyrium angustum)

Where it Grows:

- Throughout the forest, mostly in shade or semi-shade.

Tips for Identification:

- Fronds grow in asymmetrical clusters, but it sometimes grows in small groups of just 2 or 3 fronds.
- Height of fern, at maturity, can be 1 to 2 feet.
- Fern *does not* stay green in all seasons.
- Blade (the leafy part) is pointed at the tip and widest in the middle. The bottom two leaflet pairs are very variable as to whether they point down, sideways or up.
- Subleaflets are finely cut into sub-subleaflets.
- ▶ Stalk has a slight groove in the front.
- ▶ Stalk below the blade has thin scales (usually brown or black) which increase in amount closer to the ground.
- Fertile fronds, if present, have clusters of spore cases which grow on their underside and are crescent-shaped.

Can be Confused With:

- Hay-scented Fern (p. 56), which *does not* grow in clusters, but does grow in large colonies.
- Spinulose & Evergreen Wood Ferns (p. 60), which have thicker stalks which are densely covered with large light-brown scales.

Interesting Notes:

- Lady Fern is quite lacy in the beginning of the season. By the middle of summer, it looks ragged because various insects have fed on it.

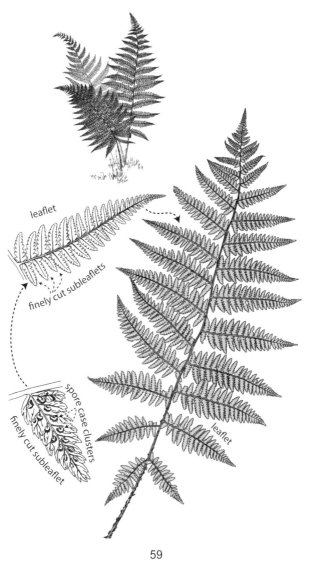

leaflet

finely cut subleaflets

spore case clusters

finely cut subleaflet

leaflet

Group 3

59

Spinulose & Evergreen Wood Fern

(Dryopteris carthusiana)   *(Dryopteris Intermedia)*

Where it Grows:

- Widespread in shaded areas, especially when wetter.

Tips for Identification:

▶ Spinulose and Evergreen Wood Ferns are look-alikes except that, on the lowest pair of leaflets, the innermost pair of subleaflets are either longer (Spinulose Wood Fern) or shorter (Evergreen Wood Fern) than the next pair.
- Fronds may grow in free-form, rather vase-like clusters.
- Height of fern, at maturity, can be 1 to 3 feet.
- Though Spinulose Wood Fern *does not* stay green in all seasons, it retains its color well after the first frost.
- Evergreen Wood Fern is evergreen and keeps dead fronds at its base. It is more common than Spinulose.
- Leaflets are pointy.
- Subleaflets are finely cut into sub-subleaflets.
▶ Stalk below the blade is densely covered with large light-brown scales.
- Fertile fronds have clusters of spore cases which grow in two rows on the underside of the subleaflets.

Can be Confused With:

- Hay-scented Fern (p. 56) stalk is brown or black, especially closer to the ground.
- Lady Fern (p. 58) stalk has thin scales (usually brown or black) which increase in number closer to the ground.

Interesting Notes:

- Florists often use the Evergreen Wood Fern in flower arrangements because it retains its shape and color.
- Contains a toxic substance that can paralyze some cold-blooded animals and some invertebrates.

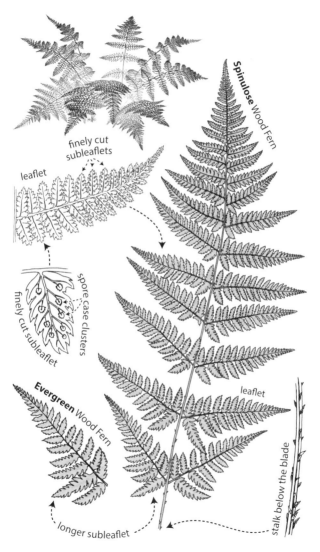

Spinulose Wood Fern

finely cut subleaflets

leaflet

spore case clusters

finely cut subleaflet

Evergreen Wood Fern

leaflet

longer subleaflet

stalk below the blade

61

Bracken Fern

(Pteridium aquilinum)

Where it Grows:
- In poor and barren soil. In sun or shade. Rarely grows in a rich site.

Tips for Identification:
- Fronds may grow in large colonies.
- ▶ Height of fern, at maturity, can be 3 to 5 feet.
- Fern *does not* stay green in all seasons.
- ▶ Blade (the leafy part) is broadly triangular.
- ▶ Blade bends almost horizontal to the ground.
- ▶ Three triangular leaflets are on separate stems.
- Fronds are thick and coarse.
- Fertile fronds, when present, have clusters of spore cases which grow on their underside, along the edge of the sub-subleaflets and are partially covered by the curled edges of those sub-subleaflets.

Can be Confused With:
- Each of the other Group 4 ferns (pp. 64-69), but they are all much smaller.

Interesting Notes:
- Poisonous to livestock.
- *Caution*: Though Bracken Fern's shoots or fiddleheads are considered a delicacy in many parts of the world, Japanese scientists have shown an association between consumption of Bracken fiddleheads and cancer of the esophagus.
- Dense understories of Bracken Fern, New York Fern or Hay-scented Fern can interfere with the regeneration of hardwood forests, threatening their sustainability.

Group 4

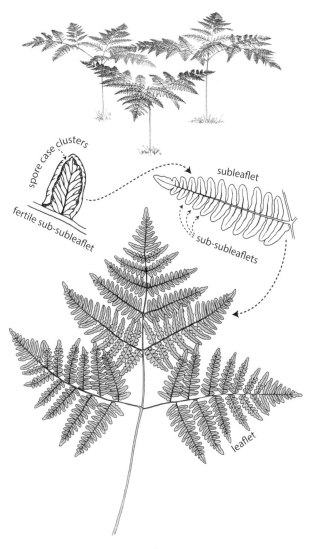

spore case clusters

subleaflet

fertile sub-subleaflet

sub-subleaflets

leaflet

63

Cut-Leaf Grape Fern

(Sceptridium dissectum)

Where it Grows:
- Can grow in partial to full sunlight.

Tips for Identification:
- Fronds *do not* grow in clusters.
- Height of fern, at maturity, can be 6 inches, except for the fertile frond which can be about 12 inches.
- Blade (the leafy part) is divided into three leaflets.
- ▶ Sterile blades are highly variable, depending upon the fineness of their cuts. Two examples of this are shown in the illustration (p. 65).
- ▶ When clusters of spore cases are present, they are in branched bead-like clusters, making the fertile portion of the frond look more like a flower.

Can be Confused With:
- Oak Fern (p. 66), which has clusters of spore cases, when present, on the underside of the blade.
- Rattlesnake Fern (p. 68), which has a fertile frond that emerges *much higher* on the stalk.
- Leathery Grape Fern (not included in this guide), which has much more rounded leaflets and subleaflets.

Interesting Notes:
- If present, new growth (the fertile portion of the frond), *emerging low to the base of the vegetative porti*on of the frond, does not appear until summer.
- The vegetative portion of the frond has a fresh green appearance, but darkens to a bronze color after several frosts. It stays this color throughout the winter and into the following spring.

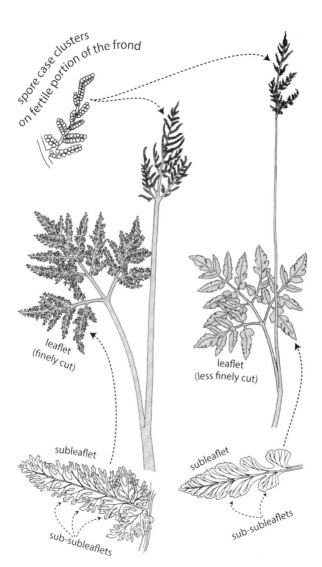

spore case clusters on fertile portion of the frond

leaflet
(finely cut)

leaflet
(less finely cut)

subleaflet

subleaflet

sub-subleaflets

sub-subleaflets

Group 4

65

Oak Fern

(Gymnocarpium dryopteris)

Where it Grows:

- Shaded places, either in soil or on rock.

Tips for Identification:

- Fronds often grow in small colonies.
- Height of fern, at maturity, can be 6 to 12 inches.
- Fern *does not* stay green in all seasons.
- ▶ Blade (the leafy part) is broadly triangular.
- ▶ Blade bends almost horizontal to the ground.
- ▶ Three triangular leaflets are on separate stems.
- Subleaflets are opposite each other and cut into sub-subleaflets.
- Some of the sub-subleaflets on the lowest pairs of subleaflets are finely cut.
- Fertile fronds, when present, have round spore case clusters growing on their underside. They are arranged in rows along the edges of the sub-subleaflets.

Can be Confused With:

- Cut-Leaf Grape Fern (p. 64), which has a fertile frond that emerges *close to the base* of the stalk.
- Rattlesnake Fern (p. 68), which has a fertile frond that emerges *high* on the stalk.

Interesting Notes:

- Oak Fern fiddleheads are produced all summer.
- Each emerging fiddlehead is divided into three ball-like parts.
- Oak Fern *is not* associated with oak trees.

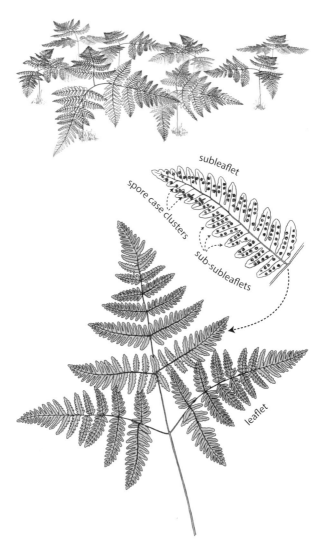

subleaflet

spore case clusters

sub-subleaflets

leaflet

Rattlesnake Fern

(Botrypus virginianus)

Where it Grows:

- Throughout the woodlands, but rarely in wetlands or on ledges.

Tips for Identification:

- Fronds *do not* grow in clusters.
- Height of fern, at maturity, can be 6 to 12 inches.
- Fern *does not* stay green in all seasons.
- ▶ Blade (the leafy part) is broadly triangular.
- ▶ Blade bends almost horizontal to the ground.
- ▶ Three triangular leaflets are on separate stems.
- Subleaflets are finely cut into sub-subleaflets.
- ▶ When clusters of spore cases are present, they are located at the tip of the fertile frond.

Can be Confused With:

- Cut-Leaf Grape Fern (p. 64), which has a fertile frond that emerges *close to the base* of the stalk.
- Oak Fern (p. 66), which has clusters of spore cases, when present, on the underside of the blade.

Interesting Notes:

- This fern gets its common name because, when it is blowing in the wind, the separate fertile frond looks like a rattlesnake's tail.

spore case clusters on fertile frond

fertile frond

leaflet

subleaflet

sub-subleaflets

Group 4

69

Maidenhair Fern

(Adiantum pedatum)

Where it Grows:

- In rich shaded soil, often with limestone bedrock.

Tips for Identification:

- Fronds may grow in scattered small clusters.
- Height of fern, at maturity, can be 6 to 18 inches.
- Fern *does not* stay green in all seasons.
- ▶ Blade (the leafy part) is fan-shaped.
- Blade bends almost horizontal to the ground.
- Blade is made up of many leaflets.
- ▶ Leaflets radiate fan-like in all directions on one side of the curving stalk.
- Subleaflets are finely cut into sub-subleaflets.
- Spore case clusters, when present, grow along the upper edges of the subleaflets.

Can be Confused With:

- There are two other rare look-alike Maidenhair Ferns.

Interesting Notes:

- Maidenhair Fern is an indicator of a rich growing site, which often has early spring wildflowers such as hepatica, ginger, leeks and Dutchman's Breeches.
- Where Maidenhair Fern grows, the trees tend to grow taller.
- The genus name of Maidenhair Fern, *Adiantum*, is derived from the Greek word *Adiantos* – meaning "unwetted" – because the leaflets repel water.
- "Maidenhair" refers to the fern's delicate hair-like appearance.

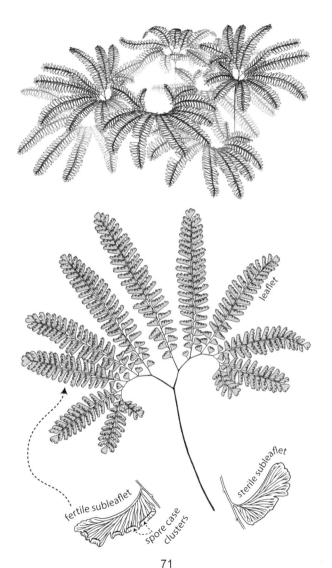

leaflet

fertile subleaflet

spore case clusters

sterile subleaflet

INDEX: COMMON FERN NAMES

INDEX: SCIENTIFIC FERN NAMES